GW00863468

Introduction.

In a world of constant change, in a world that in some respects is coming apart at the seams. It is important to have points of reference, heroes who seem to exemplify the values and principles that we (the people of today) identify with. To quote Jeb Barlet (from the west wing).

"I want to be the guy, you want to be guy counts on" (Sorkin, 2003)

There are many "big names" or people of note throughout the medieval period that have stories that cast them in a good light or bad. But the truth is often so far more interesting.

"I looked to find examples on the field of chivalry And I saw mighty arms much stronger than my arms could ever be, So I thought perhaps that field was not for me" (Dale, 2006)

Authority in the medieval period had to be decentralized and distributed. This was to make sure that if there was an issue or problem was mitigated and solved quickly. Communication over a long distance is hard, and basic skills like reading and writing are rare or non-existent in some sections of society.

They pair this with the need to protect land, resources and people from attack, to foster resources to trade, and to maintain the working population. The reaction to these needs for the high medieval period is feudalism.

The leadership of the so-called feudal system is based on the concept of partial symbiosis between a lord and a person who provides services to a

Vasal. At scale (when we increase the size of a system), this creates a hierarchical system.

This breaks down because of the massive abuses of people using their positions to advance their own and family agenda and social positions. Some lords show narcissistic tendencies, or are completely unfit for the position they hold.

The weakness of several kings, who were the wrong person, in the wrong position at the wrong time, do not assist the issues mentioned. To this mess comes the main character of this book, Andrew Harcla.

We can talk of the examples, persons like King Steven, King John and must relevant too is talking here Edward II. Feudalism is a difficult thing to control in practice as the one hallmark is that a Lord has near absolute control over the land they are invested with.

But why write a book about a forgotten traitor? I hear you cry, because in a world where you can only evaluate a person by their actions, we need Heroes who are not heroic because they were successful (whatever that means). but are Heroic because they define the Mantra "Deeds not Words".

Chapter 1, The world that was.

To review a society in history, one needs to look in some detail at the many elements of a society. It is also important to create a framework to ensure one is providing the required information to people.

One way of looking at a society is as a living organism, so here I will borrow the mnemonic device of Mrs Gren from Biology, to talk about each point. Mrs Gren refers to the seven processes that all living things share.

Movement.

Here I will describe how people could move around England. Moving around England is "hard" for many people and would take much longer than it would today. There were two primary methods of travel. Roads and waterways.

Roads

They used roads in the medieval period, and they built the best ones on the old roman networks, but because Rome took its technology and expertise when they "pulled out" in the 4th century, the roads created were of a lesser quality. They also considered the maintenance and building of roads important, as they would need it for the movement of the armies and trade.

The problem is that roads are dangerous; as banditry is a constant issue on the roads, as outlaws and footpads are endemic. Travelers on the road would have also had to contend with the terrain and weather, along with carrying everything with them.

To combat these issues, very often people would band together into small groups and some wealthy people would travel with protection, whether this was a mercenary or knight.

With the number of issues surrounding traveling long distances on the roads, it can be limited by traveling with a group and carrying protection. There are also added problems with some roads being impassable for sometimes years. These issues are made double when moving cargo.

Waterways

Waterway refers to the inlets, streams, rivers and other waterways that boats and ships can navigate. This method of travel is far less taxing on the person and a person is more protected from criminality. A boat will also enable one to move people and resources more easily by road.

There are also some issues. The security and comfort used for travel comes at a premium cost, which can be set by the boat owner. Some people would have their own boats, most didn't.

However, there are some significant challenges that need to be overcome to use the waterways effectively. First is that the crew needs to have a knowledge of the Individual waterways, each there individual aspects that may endanger the boat.

The water offers the ability to move cargo between centers of trade and markets as most cities were built near a flowing water source. This had the effect of having.

Respire.

In this section, I am going to talk about the fostering of resources and the application of their resources to the projects and needs of the county.

From the retraction and the eventual fall of the Western Roman Empire, this left power vacuum is left and without the support of the Roman Empire, the tribes, clans and groups compete for resources.

Medieval society had a different interpretation of work and labor, while some work was paid for most was in creating staples such as food. In this case, remuneration came though being able to keep anything over a certain level.

The King is arguably (Investiture Controversy) the highest point of authority in the feudal system of England, as from the reign of William I (the Conquer) the lands are owned (by right of conquest) by the kings of England.

Because it is not possible for the king to hold, administer and control the kingdom of the size and complexity of England, of the size of England, on his own he has to trust lords to act in his stead (social and legal) they will support the king in war, the collection of tax and in the political acts that the Monarch undertakes.

These Priceable lords are referred to as the 'tenants in chief' or earls, who intrust their tenant lords and barons. Who intrust vassal lords (these lords had several titles). It is important here to say that phases change depending on the time and 'system' we are talking about, e.g. count are things just not in England.

A common thread to many of the lords is their Knightly training, because of the practical need for military protection and organization.

The Freemen were those people who are capable of self support though skilled labor or trading. While slavery had been abolished in the christian world by the church, the social and economic conditions meant people could not support themselves.

The Church is a social group of people who are connected to the Church of Rome, from 1066 there is a much stronger dogmatic protection to the church. The church expresses an independence of policy and legal process, in Which has its own laws and procedures.

Sense.

The ability to sense risks and danger is important to ensure the safety of the whole. In this section, we can discuss how the system looked and acted to ensure the safety of the whole.

The requirement to trust the person next to you in a battle was considered being extremely important, as this person would act in the lord's stead. To assist the lord in their administration, there would be several people who would specialize in the many areas, such as Law, Tax and the enforcement of the lord's will.

Decision making was, to a large part, local and left to a combination of unwritten and written laws, traditions and decisions made by the local lord. However, if a decision is made further up the "feudal chain" then the local lord has to change their mind.

In war, local lords call on their own knights, soldiers and lesser lords, however there was also a general levy for men capable of fighting being marched to war, but these levied troops would be considered, as last ditch troops for both combat and economic reasons. Because of requirements of Medieval Combat and campaign, the ability of a Levied person to dig ditches and Trenches to support and assist the fighting men was more important.

Grow.

Growth in the medieval period is misunderstood by popular history, because it is a common method to use the guide markers of development of technology to measure the growth of a society.

However, while there are technological improvements to items, the greatest growth is the development of systematic social and or government process improvements that may be called the building blocks of England.

While there is a fair augment, later ages define the ideas that heavily attract attention and thought of today. It is the progress of the medieval period that provides the underpins for these ideas.

Governance.

The medieval period shows the greatest changes in government. When William the Conqueror reforms the English government (December 1066), it differs greatly from the government that ruled at the end of the War of the Roses.

But this process of improvement is conducted through bloody and brutal warfare. however, in this mud and blood of the battlefield, the cut and thrust of intrigue, we see the first vestiges of law, the first checks on royal power, through the Balances of parliament's "advice", and the court systems.

Law, and legal process.

While has been used more recently to moderate and control problematic behavior, law as a system guidance has grown from being the means by which the king's will is disseminated there "will" (what the kings wants to do), and grows to be the system that is used to check and create fairness in society.

It is also important to note that over some 800 years, ideals of fairness have changed. Social structure was extremely important in the period.

Just as the civil court of England still sees cases that are arguments between two or more parties, many of the functional aspects of evidence, witness and make your case to an independent person. Empowered to enforce the means of their judgment is important to civility even today.

Reproduce

For the 'self-worth' of a society, country, kingdom or other state is important to expand its lands, peoples, influence and power. One also needs to maximize their resource potential. For England, this turns into the repeated wars with Scotland, Ireland, Wales, and France In order to expand.

Excrete.

The Excretion of the society is how that society deals with internal elements that have become problematic and or toxic. This can take different forms, of which are criminality, social exhaustivity.

In contrast to our methods of dealing with criminals and those deemed undesirable, Medieval English society had a unique way of handling them. They would hold individuals accused of a crime until the trial and the judge makes their decision.

The Excretion of the society is how that society deals with internal elements. This can take different forms, of which are criminality, social exhaustivity.

In contrast to our methods of dealing with criminals and those deemed undesirable, Medieval English society had a unique way of handling them. They would hold individuals accused of a crime until the trial and the judge makes their decision.

They make the Punishments to fit the crime. We would consider the methods brutal. One can divide the punishment into three groups.

- Fines
- Physical Punishments
- Capital Punishments

In a Very Practical way compared to Europe, India and Asia, England is an island, and a part of Ireland is the last land to the west. Which has benefits and huge weaknesses. This is enhanced by some Dogmatics of the Church. This had massive effects on the communities that were not part of the majority, or the empowered.

Nutrition.

Unlike today, famine is not rare in England, and even most of England's workforce is directed at raising crops. While the lower orders would live on a vegetarian diet, they could improve this through rabbits, wild birds and other wildlife. As you move up, though, the social structure, meat and spices are more of a choice, and or a political necessity.

There is also the social nutrition, much of which is administered by the church. The church was not a question or debate but an absolute, a certainty in a world of fear where each day could be the last.

Chapter 2, A Quick history.

England and Scotland have a long and complex history, a history that is splattered in blood, intrigue and injustice on both sides. This complexity continues to be reflected in the politics of the two counties today. This deeply emotive subject needs to be understood before one can understand the world of Andrew Harclay.

On the morning of 19th, March 1286, King Alexander III of Scotland is found dead after being thrown from his horse, after attempting to ride through the storm to his wife. However, Alexander III died without leaving someone to take up the crown, his own son having died on the 28th January 1284 at 20. The next in line is now Margaret, the maid of Norway, born 1283. Margaret is Alexander III's granddaughter.

Two weeks later Alexander II (the father of Alexander III) called a meeting of Senior Church officers and Nobles at Scone, where he issued the "tailzie" which confirms Margaret as the rightful hair.

However, on more practical terms, Margaret is only four years old and is in Norway, with very little political support in Scotland. With a number, claimants come out of the woodwork, because "only a king makes a king" and a council of nobles and church officers reaches for help from the King of Norway (Haakon V Magnusson) and the King of England (Edward the First)

King Haakon, who was King of Norway from 1299 until 1319, but distracted by internal issues. The king of England from 1237 to 1307. Edward I called together a council made of legal experts, magnates and lords in both the "English system" and the "Scottish system". However, there are only two "real" parties that can take and hold the throne of Scotland.

A party led by John Balliol, and a party led by Robert the Bruce. The make up of the council constitutional experts selected by Edward as arbitrator, and the two dominant parties.

Edward selects twenty-five people, Robert selects forty and John selects forty. After two years of debate, the council returns to Edward saying that the rightful legal king of England is John Balliol, Edward agrees. However, there is a growing problem: in a monarchy, the powers of the state flows (or rolls) from a sovereign, especially in terms of authority.

Because the Scottish throne is vacant, the vital duties go undone. One of the most important is the addressing of grievances. To find a solution to this, Edward directed the English court to hear about Scottish cases. The English courts stopped taking fresh cases when John Balliol was made King (17 November 1292) and still heard the cases.

The lords of Scotland were very opposed to what the Scottish lords felt was English Interface, and once crowned, applied huge amounts of pressure to distance himself from the court of Edward. To Edward, the rule of law had to be maintained even at the temporary discomfort of Scottish nobility.

But the council would settle on the claim of John Balliol, using the right of 'primogeniture' because of the closest male relation to Alexander III. Edward I made the announcement in the castle of Berwick upon tweed on the 17 November 1292. With the matter settled, Edward ensured John became king on 30 November 1292.

Edward at this point is fighting in France. John and the court reach out to Philip IV (king of France) to make a treaty and begin negotiating in 1295. When news of the plan reaches Edward I, He leaves his army under a captain and rides for the English-Scottish border.

While Travelling through England, Edward calls on lords not in France to join him and starts gathering forces, he sends the bulk of his forces to Monkchester (called Newcastle today) and some to Carlisle.

With Scotland in the north having a treaty with France in the south, Edward's fear is that he will have to fight a war on two fronts, a thousand miles apart.

Edward reaches out to John to negotiate. He sends a letter with an opening offer and waits for a response, but none comes. Edward moves to Monkchester and they attack Carlisle on 26 March 1296, which is relieved when Edward Marches on Scotland.

The offer sent to John is to stop the English army from invading. Is to give Edward the castle at Roxburgh, Jedburgh, and Berwick.

When this formal begins the Scottish wars of independence, Edward marches over the border and crosses the river tweed on the 28th March 1296 and then heads for Coldstream priory. The army stops at Coldstream for the night.

The next morning, the army makes for Berwick the trading port for Scotland, which was garrisoned. William the Hardy, Lord of Douglas, commands the company at Berwick. Robert de Clifford, 1st Baron de Clifford, led English forces. Robert sets his forces loose on the town and then invests the castle with a siege.

William Surrenders and marches the Castles company away, the sack of Berwick's death rate at between seven and fourteen thousand. This is the first blow to Edwards' advance.

Edward spends a month creating a Strongpoint to cover his back, and a supply base. It was during this time that John broke his oath of peace with England. Edward moves to take the castle at Dunbar a few miles up the coast. Edward sent a potent force of knights led by one his best (and John's father-in-law) John de Warenne, 6th Earl of Surrey, to lay siege to the castle.

The defenders of the castle at Dunbar led by Patrick, Earl of March's, sent letters to John for aid who moved his arm to relieve the castle, but met the English army on 27 April 1296.

The importance of the knight.

A knight is a hard to idea to talk about in today's world because the responsibility and the duties performed by a knight are directly tied to the economic and military needs of the time. As stated before, the 'command-and-control systems' were decentralised.

The reality of the pre-medieval and early medieval periods meant that life is harder and more dangerous in ways that are hard to explain. Warfare for both power and resources is commonplace and normalised. This predicated the need for lords that could fight and fight well to protect their lands. By the ninth century, much of the coastal population would know the panic-inducing fear of square sailed ships.

These raiders, sometimes referred to as Vikings, would start with the attack on Lindisfarne. But soon, they would make their way up the many waterways to strike deep within lords' lands. The Saxons would respond to this by creating the feuds. A system reminiscent of the old West, the feuds, was functionally a "posy" of all fight men to deal with the invaders. Which has its own set of strengths and weaknesses.

The system was excellent at establishing how people were needed to respond to an issue, and it was a good way of assembling a large force quickly. But there was no way of controlling the quality of the army that responded. There is also limited specialty in the forces.

The raiders were a highly mobile force that would implement hit-and-run tactics, but over time, other horse people would arrive and begin to trade and colonise areas of England. With this much "slower" method, the small task forces of motivated, well armed and trained would outfight the Saxons.

However, the Saxons would learn from this and would incorporate trained well-armed men that were on "standby". Over time, these would be called the housecarls, while some might think that these are (or better than knights). But knights came over with the Norman invasion. The professionalisation that was created by creating the housecarls would improve combat effectiveness and would nip some issues before they would become large scale.

This hybrid system would continue until the Norman invasion of 1066, and introducing Norman feudalism to England. The battle of Hastings decimated the "ruling class" of Saxon England. And many of Saxon lords after this were minor lords that quickly (over the next five years) were replaced or became very norman.

With this comes the Norman knights who are entrusted with land (the knight's fee), and begin making permanent changes. The knight remains the standing (in terms of leadership and capability) fighting force, definitely the coming of the Black Death 1348 - 1349. Some argument has been made that the last of the "noble" fighting were the pike blocks of the English civil war. (of which I cry that gunpowder ruins everything and I change the subject).

At its worst, the knights were an old boys' club, not unlike "posh" boarding schools today. But at its best, knighthood was a brotherhood, a mixture of adventure and "daring dos".

Chapter 3, Andrew's Family's Background.

Andrew was born around the year 1270, to Micheal and Joan FitzJohn, the daughter of the wealthy, landowning family. Micheal was like many knights of the age, invested and entrusted to serve and protect their lord.

Sir Micheal de Harcla

In the Case of Sir Micheal, he is a retainer for Robert Clifford. The Lord Clifford operated under the peerage of the Baron de Clifford. The Clifford Family had originally come over as a member of the army of William the Conqueror in 1066. And settled at Clifford Castle in Herefordshire.

The Peerage was created in 1299, as Baron De Clifford, and suited the newly minted Earl Marshal, Robert, and was killed at the Battle of Bannockburn. Baron de Clifford would also have extensive lands and responsibilities, which included Appleby Castle, Westmoreland, and was the Feudal Lord for Skipton (Yorkshire).

This is further added to when The King (Edward I) makes Robert the first 'Lord Warden of the Marches'. This meant that Roger was the Military commander for the border with Scotland. A sleepy far flung reward, it was not as there had been an extended cold war between the two kingdoms.

In a legal court case enacted, to claim a manner, Micheal lists his own ancestral line from the time of Edward I to the time of Henry I as seen, in the Family tree above.

Joan FitzJohn

On Andrew's Maternal Side of the Family; His mother, Joan FitzJohn, was born in 1260. Joan was born to William Fitz John, a wealthy landowner in the county of Yorkshire.

Joan was born in the Village of Hartley in Westmorland and married in St Stephen's church in Kirby Steven in 1275.

Marriages in medieval England.

One of the many aspects of medieval society is that marriages were very often not for love but to create a connection between two noble families, to use the metaphor of the social ladder. One way of progressing one's family though the social structures is through marrying well.

While it was wise to marry for the gain of one's family, not for oneself (love), much is made in the song and poems of the travelling troubadours of courtly love, also forbidden love.

The power dynamics.

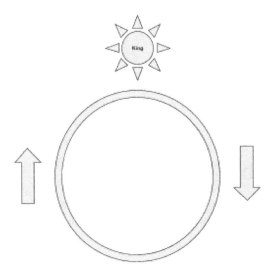

The image above is a simplified version of a concept known as a wheel of fate. The Centre of power, (in this case the king) is at the top of the wheel and people at the royal court and in society are somewhere on the wheel but can be divided into two rough groups, the group that is in favour and those who are falling from favour.

The Brothers and sisters

Before moving on to the brothers and sisters of Andrew, while it is normal to have a large family (complained to today), The Office of national statistics sets the number of children at 1.92 (2020).

Back in the medieval period, a bigger family provided a level of security, due to the number of reasons. One reason is the infant mortality. This is paired with the need to both create a firm power base in a highly patriarchal society, and prevent a noble family from dying out. In the medieval period, this gave rise to the adage, "the hair, the spare, and a third for the Church".

It is very light that Andrew had many more siblings than have been recounted here, but it is unlikely these children reached adulthood. It is possible that some children were lost in the "mists of time". Andrew had a brother and two sisters.

Henry Harclay

A younger brother to Andrew, Henry, who had found fair fame, all of his own, John was a master of philosophy at the now legendary establishment of Oxford. Born around c1270 and passed away on 25th June 1317.

Henry became a Master of the Arts, at the very young age of twenty-six, and in the same year was appointed (1296) rector of the church at Dacre on the 25th of December 1296. But remains a secular theologian until Henry is ordained as a priest 1297.

Henry attended the university of Paris between 1300 to 1310, when Henry finished his studies in Paris and returned to his 'Alma mater' Oxford and was declared a master of theology c1312, In the same year made the Chancellor of the University of Oxford.

Henry Harclay, did not rest on his position, and is very active in the role and attentive in maintaining and extending rights of Oxford, which put him at odds with the local Dominicans, when Edward II decree that the mayor of Oxford is to allow the officers of the university to "test" the beer. Such is the nature of the resulting disagreement that Henry would be required to defend them at the papal courts (in Avignon) repeatedly, and attempts to hammer out an agreement, but dies on a trip to Avignon in 1317.

Henry was a Titan of Philosophy of his own time, being a graduate of the mighty universities of Both Oxford and Paris would have ensured that he was at the very height of his powers and the strong connection and feeling duty to Oxford must be a family trait.

Isabel Vernon,

Isabel was born around 1261, but when the king took the lands Michael (Harcla) de Harcla in 1278 and Isabel was made a ward of the king and married her too, Richard de Vernon (1267 to 1296).

Sarah de Leybourne

Sarah was born around the year of 1292, in the family Seat of Hartley Castle, a walking distance from the Village of Kirkby Stephen. She was married to Robert (Leybourne) de Leybourne and had one child (who survived to adulthood) Thomas Musgrave and died after 1327, around the age of 35, in Westmoreland.

History has been extremely hard on women, and the lack of detail of the lives above is because it has proved difficult to find information on these people, And while new insightful scholarly work has started to lift the lid on Women in the Medieval period. I would not guess the lives they had, But it is Women who did the 'Hard Graft', ensuring that Castles, houses and people are cared for, fed and or watered. there is abundance of evidence that society would have ground to halt.

Chapter 4, The Family Seat

There is an old saying that "for the English every home is his castle", This is Partly true, because like many Minor Knightley families they were entrusted with a small "castle", This type of fortifications can be considered to be a so-called fortified Manor.

Information on Castles.

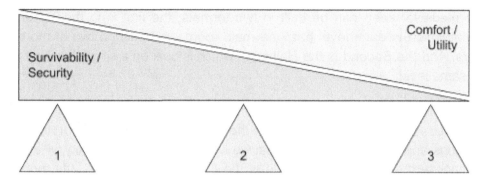

When it comes to Castles and fortifications in a General way all castles exist in a continuum between being able to survive in extreme situations such as siege. And people have a comfortable life in the castle.

In this frame of thought, we can group medieval castles in to three groups;

1. **Full Castles,** These are the backbone of the defense of England, this type of castle designed to hold together while being attacked. This type of castle is normally used when fortifying key points, Some examples are the Tower of London, New- castle (Monkchester) and Carlisle.
2. **Local Castle,** these are much smaller castles, that most often are a keep, and a fence at most.
3. **The Manors** which are the most comfortable of the fortifications, and many became the official homes to minor lords and officials.

Most medieval castles are made up of a number of elements, The Primary Element of every castle is the keep. Which is the main "strongpoint", the second are the supportive defenses, In the many cases these are lesser Strong Points (which can be a tower or a gatehouse) and walls, and a number of more complex defenses.

The Keep

The medieval keep can be built in two formats, the first is in the Tower, format which is each level has one main room, and built on two or more floors. And the Second is the Hall type, which is built on a single level with the same level.

The Main rooms and the common rooms that keep have the Hall and the Chamber. The Hall is very much the use for everything from trials, meetings and feasts, and events that we would use in a community, village or other large space. The Second is the Chamber which is a little more private space. Normally this is where lord can talk to his friends and 'experts' about decisions.

Gatehouses

The other smaller 'standpoints' are the gate used to provide structural and defensive support and an additional protection for gate or ports of entry.

Walls

Walls are important and provide much of the security of an area. By their height and their ability to control access to an area but require both people and resources to defend and maintain.

The land itself.

When the last Great glacial ice age comes to end, And the greater ice shelf proceeds towards Carlisle, Which leaves a green and pleasant landBut soon Life will start to spring forward.

Hartley is always very closely associated with the fate of the land around itIt has been invaded by the Romans and then abandoned by the Romans,

Leaving the local client nations to pick up the pieces however to go into this history would detract from other sections in this book.

Hartley castle.

The Seat of the De Hartley Family since the building of the first castle, in the small village of Harley, just to the east of the town of Kirby Steven.

Like many of the small castles, much of the original buildings are lost to time; what remains is some earthworks and the fragments of buildings. They lost this manner as part of the decimation of Andrew and his household.

An Image of Hartley Castle circa 1600

Almost none of the castle remains and the majority of the site was redeveloped by the 18 century. Today the land is still used in a private Capacity. Much of the castle has been lost. But above is an Image made in the 1600.

The area around it.

The first people to know the land that would later be known as Heartly were the neolithic peoples, some two thousand five hundred years ago, these people would first be nomadic and settle in land.

These peoples would be invaded by the SPOR also known as Rome, and would become known through the writing of Claudius Ptolemy and others as the Carvetii.

These people would align with Rome becoming a 'clent tribe', When the Romans left in the 4th Century. When the Romans left there was absolute chaos in England, the many different tribes who had become dependent on Rome's merchant system. Would have to find new and or different ways of supporting themselves.

This is where the small kingdoms would be set up and fall, and would become part of the Celtic kingdom of Strathclyde. This was until the 7th century when Saxon (Northumbria) forces invaded and took the area of modern day Penrith. This places the family seat just about on the border between Northumbria and Strathclyde.

The kingdom of Strathclyde was then invaded and "shattered" by an invasion of Norsemen from Ireland in 870. But this invasion was short lived as the land was bought into the kingdom of Scotland.

Chapter 5 Andrew

Born in around 1270, to Micheal and Joan, a 'minor' knightly family, Andrew was probably born in the family seat of Hartley castle. This is due to Micheal being entrusted with land to fund, his needs and Joan would be running the household. Andrews' early years would have been normal for time.

Such is the style of the time, Andrew would have nurses and nannies, until the age of around five. At five he would start to spend time with other knights' children.

Page

Knightly children would be taught many of the soft skills that would be needed later, but no military training, **yet** . Loyalty and trust were extremely important and though having a long standing relationship does help with this.

At the age of around seven Andrew would have been sent to the household of a more senior knight, in the case of Andrew it is lightly that this would be sent to the household of lord Clifford. Who was Micheal's "Boss" (superior).

This is for a number of reasons, the primary reason was that the children of the knightly families would need to work together in a battle and on campaign, and because so much of knights "duty" is concerned in close combat, synergy is very important.

A secondary reason is that the training as a "unit" is Standardized within that unit. There is also a need to ensure that the fighting class is correctly trained. These children would be referred to as pages.

These children would receive an education meant to knock everyone down to the same level, literally cleaning out horses, soul rending back breaking work. Which may have had two reasons.

The first is training the body, being a knight for the amount of time required for a knight to be active is a physically demanding job. For the armor, the weapons. Because a knight would be required to go toe to toe with other knights they had to be able to go the distance, not just physically but cognitively.

The pages would learn how to be a knight, by learning how to serve at table, and by assisting the staffing of the castle would learn how a castle was run. I Knight may not always have servants and or attendants to help maintain his equipment, so he need to know how to look after it.

As a page progressed they would be introduced to hunting, and familiarity with differently knightly weapons. Should the Page show some promise at around the age of fourteen they would become a Squire.

Squire

A Squire which is taken from medieval French meaning "shield bearer" (in 1635 the vocabulary of the french language was modernized). The focus of the training is now turned towards war.

Weighted weapons would be 'introduced', and you again the philosophy of learning through practice is the order of the day. A squire's main duties would be the cleaning and maintaining of weapons, armor and equipment. Being "trusted" to look after much more expensive horses.

A classic training montage of a 14 year old boy sticking a Pell[1] with a heavy wooden sword, these weapons (like the romans) would be weighted with lead to make it heavier to ensure that the squire could fight well. there

---

[1] A type of striking post for practicing cuts, and drills

was also the idea for a False sword which is a sword that was not-sharpened, so the Squire would learn how steel works (vs wood)

Squires would be permitted to go on campaign with the knight, who would have one or two with him. And their job is to act as the road crew. Looking after knight's stuff. Securing loot, provisions and prisoners.

All being well by twenty one would be knighted, it is important to note that not everyone who started up on the path to be a knight, would end up being knighted, as maybe the funding would not hold out or fate would intervene.

Knighting.

Not unlike graduating University or getting that dream job, this event will be what people have been working towards for 15 years. The bruises, cracked bones, fractures, spat blood, the humiliation and the small victories.

Receiving a knighthood must be very special, as I have said before at their best the knights were a brotherhood, thus a knighthood also held a pseudo-religious element.

Unlike the formal rinse and repeat dubbing of today, the complex ceremony of the accolade, (which would raise and remake the candidate to be a knight). The ceremony sees a huge amount of variances between places.

but each part of the ceremony has an important meaning to the people involved. In some cases the candidate would have to wear a special uniform, in some cases this would mean that the candidate would need to wear hoes of a special color (for example brown and green, to represent the land they will be trusted to protect.). in some cases a red surcoat (which represents the blood that they will spill for their lord).

Once that knight has been knighted, this is the point where they are going to be the most aggressive as in today's jobs market as a young knight who did not have an established "pathway". would have build a CV of doing stupidly brave, bravely stupid things.

In this we can turn to the Legendy History of Sir William Marshall, who "cut his teeth in the Torny Circuit. competing in competitions to make a name.

Andrew's early Military Career.

There is not much written directly about Andrew's early career but it is probable that Andrew would at least travel and take part in tournaments. to gain experience with different knights and techniques, while considered a sport the tournaments is a good way of gaining experience in a simulation of warfare.

But by 1307 Andrew must have and started to make a name for himself in the local area. The time Andrew is talked about in the records we have was in 1292.

This was because he attained the Westmoreland "traveling court" also known as Eyre. He is thought to be around 21 years of age.

Just because Andrew appears to have been in attendance. But there should be no assumption that Andrew was involved as the attendance at the court would have been part of the life that a family would have.

Chapter 6 Active Duty

Andrew's first formal campaign was in 1304 where he served in the Scottish wars of independence. Where he is instructed to assist Robert de Clifford. In defending the Anglo Scottish border from Scottish aggression.

Lord Robert was warden of the northern role, a role that granted him the command of all English forces in the border area.

The Background.

The background to this war is that the Scottish king Alexander III died without hare, this is where a collection of Scottish lords and Bishops came together to prevent the "Anarchy" (this is also the name of the wars resulting from Henry I death) that a civil war would bring. There would be many who would claim the Scottish Throne.

The closest person that could technically take the throne is the maid of Norway, but there was but was not a viable option.

But due to social and civil values of the time "only a king could make a king" and these lords had candidates they could turn to; the first is the king of Norway, who was imbued with his own problems. Which left the King of England, Edward I.

This is where the situation gets politically complicated, the situation has been made so by people who take a more "more moden" view. The thing is that the people of Scotland and the people of England, lived under a system that is influenced by the doctrine of the "great chain of Being". With a government that is built from the ideals that there must be a single leader.

Once Edward had been empowered to act in scotland by the Scottish magnates he put together a great council of legal, constitutional, scottish experts. The council was made up of 104 auditors.

Edward then asked both Robert the Bruce and John Balliol to find 40 Electors, while Edward would find 24 electors all of whom were taken from the political life of scotland.

The council would meet for the first time on the 17th of November 1292 and after many hours of debate the council came to the conclusion that John Balliol should be the next king.

Because Edward had been made in effect the Lord protector of the realm in scotland. This meant that English courts could hear Scottish cases.

This continued but a decision was made when John was made king that English courts would not be able to take new cases, but the courts to continue to process the cases already accepted.

As the court was being used as the court of the last result. There was no court to hear the cases, "Justice must be done, and seen to be done".

Under a massive amount of political pressure to put 'distance' between himself and Edward, John's hand is forced but there is a huge risk, John knows that Edward is a good military commander with an army that has Repeatedly taken on defeated Scottish armies before.

To ensure that Edward cannot threaten Scotland John Reaches out to Edward's other friend/enemy france. The idea was that if Scotland was attacked the French could also provide military support, Sandwiching England between the two.

This was of interest to the french king as he was in a Intermittent war with Edward, on receiving word of the negotiation Edward would leave the war in France. While moving though England. Edward is calling a second army to act as a 'threat' to John and Scotland.

Edward at this point was sending letters, his commanders and forces gathered in Monkchester (now called Newcastle). At the same time a number of letters were sent to John, this was an attempt to prevent war.

as with most negotiations there was an opening offer. This time there was a demand for a number of castles, of various types. John's response was an invasion and an assault on Carlisle.

On the 26th of March 1296 a Scottish army led by John Comyn, Earl of Buchan came across the border and attacked Carlisle. The City withstood four days of siege. And was forced to withdraw as on the 28th of March. The English Army lead by By Edward I crossed the river Tweed and marched on Berwick upon Tweed.

Doing his part.

While it is very lightly that Andrew was involved in some way, however any leadership positions he would have taken were not until 1304. Where he received instructions to assist Baron De Clifford with the defenses of the north of England.

The context for this is that from march 1296 Edward I had invaded Scotland and while the truth of history is far more complex than "Edward Bad" it is beyond the scope of this book. Scotland officially had fallen quite quickly but there was substantial resistance.

He seems to be extremely good at this as his standing in local affairs Improved his position, As in the year of 1311 he was appointed to the Position that his father held, the Sheriff of Cumberland.

In the background of all of this a pseudo peace, and while a strong military presence, and political situation had pushed Robert the Bruce into hiding. But Robert is not idle, Robert earlier defeats and stripped much of the "fair weather support" and left a small highly loyal and motivated force.

Robert starts using a fast moving asymmetric warfare taskforce and quickly starts taking back castles held by English Allies and English lords.

Followed was Further accolades As in the following year He was elected as night of the shire (1312). In his first major campaign of 1313 he distinguished himself in the defense against the Scottish invasion. And again in 1315 When he defended himself against Robert the Bruce When defending Carlisle from siege.

Chapter 7 Bannockburn

"Oh how the mighty fall" (King James Bible), To the Medieval mind warfare in the open field, also known as the pitched battle, was extremely risky and a single battle could change everything and at Bannockburn Robert the Bruce and an army of Scots did just that.

"Join the Scottish revolution

Freedom must be won by blood

Now we call for revolution

Play the pipes and cry out loud" (Sabaton, 2018)

Robert had built from nothing an army able for taking of the english in the field, he had retaken castles and pushed the english out of scotland, however the long shadow of King Edward I had died leaving his son Edward II to take on the affairs of england.

Edward II was unpopular with the English nobility. And the focus was removed from scotland, Robert not being idle consolidates his hold on Scotlands and though defeating his largest threat.

Once this had been done, King Robert and started taking back major castles, that were the English Strongs and by the spring of 1314 and the taking of Roxburgh only the imposing fortresses of Bothwell and Sterling were holding out.

Robert left the siege in the hands of his brother and marched south, to meet the English Army. what came on was a massive army the full weight of the english state. But this was not the united disciplined army.

Strictly speaking there is no record of what Andrew was doing on the two days of fierce combat, but it is lightly that Andrew was with his feudal lord Robert de clifford. We know the Baron De Cliffed died, in a cavalry charge on the second day.

Robert the Bruce, had trained his army with care and understood the ground he was fighting on and united his kingdom behind him. To his troops he was a proven commander, with the ability to lead.

Edwards was nothing like his father, but it can be argued no-one should be. Edward was not liked, for many reasons. Some would call attention to Piers Gaveston, and this exacerbates the issues Edward had in his court. It was the inactiveness in handling state affairs. Nevertheless the events of scotland's ment that Edward II.

This can be seen as the flash point which started the brush fires that would be eventually brought to pass, first very public removal of a Monarch from the throne of England.

Despite much of popular history the battle itself was fought by two competent commanders, both of whom made sensible tactical decisions based on the best understanding of the field they had.

Robert vs Edward II

Robert had built the core of his army himself, and carefully trained them to fight in close formation to defeat the Heavy Cavalry Charge, the Schiltron.

The Schiltron is a formation of close packed men with "pikes" and all types of polearms. This formation ment as long as the formation held there nerve and held together no Cavalry charge could touch them. Additionally the length of the pike meant any Infantry would have a hard time making any progress. Because Robert grew up and trained with exposure to anglo norman society and methods of warfare. At the same time Robert's forces were united and the majority of lords of Scotland had given them to robert.

Edward II on the otherhad had a massive army, but was split along many lines, and commanded by lords that were a hair's width away from rebelling.

While the army could be considered the full strength of England, the question would clearly be whether the English knights and lords trusted the command of Edward II there were being given by their king. The battle was a close run thing, and to summarize was an example of technology, numbers vs discipline and good leadership.

The Battle.

As can be seen from the pie chart below, England had a massive numerical advantage over the Scottish Forces, The Scottish Army numbered between 5,000 - 8,000, the English force numbering between 20 and 25,000.

These numbers are frighteningly large, with a ratio of around 4 to 1. On paper the English will dominate the battlefield. with horse, archers and Infantry.

But Robert had a tactic that would win the battle, this was the use of the Schiltron formation. Robert split his much smaller army into three "divisions"'. one division was commanded by Robert himself, Second was commanded by Robert's Brother, and lastly led by the "black" douglas. But unlike when the formation was used by William Wallace these Schiltron could move.

Commpassion of Scotland vs England forces

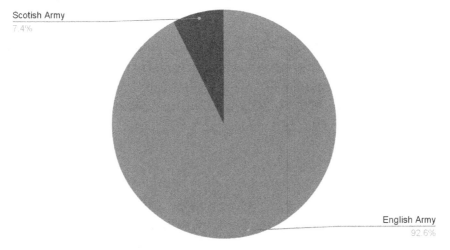

Scotish Army
7.4%

English Army
92.6%

The Schiltron is a military field formation that makes best use of the polearms, spears and Lances essentially making a wall of "things that a pokey" in the case of both bannockburn and Williams Walace's earlier battle at Falkirk they used Circular Schiltrons these were extremely effective when fighting the Heavy Cavalry of the english. These Schiltrons had two weaknesses, they relied on the troop "standing" (some or all of the troop not running away) and they were extremely susceptible to mass archery.

The formation was extremely effective at bannockburn and broke the back of the english army, the defeat was extremely hard fought, and the routing of the english army. Which started when Edward II with a group of five hundred fled.

Leaving his force in the field. Leaving a huge number of English dead and among the twisted and broken dead was Robert Clifford, 1st Baron Clifford along with many others.

There is some evidence to suggest Andrew was at the battle and he survived. A group made their way back to Carlisle. But much of the surviving army made it back to Berwick-upon-tweed and then Newcastle.

The effects of the defeat at bannockburn, were felt extremely deeply throughout England with the death of the Baron de Clifford, the local court and political life would have been put into Chaos.

Andrew returns to his role as an Military Commander for carlisle and starts a program of insuring the defense of carlisle for the coming attack.

Chapter 8 the Military build up

To understand the military build up and the siege of 1315, one has to understand the background to the larger battles. From the year of 1311 there had been a number of Raids into the North of England.

But while the walls of Carlisle held strong, the Garrison was small at 14 men (4 men at arms and 10 Archers). The Sheriff was only given £20 per year for the defense of the county. This was until August 1311 and the Scottish attack on Gilsland. Andrew was made sheriff of Cumberland in October 1311.

Because of the attack on Carlisle's Garrison 8 knights, 156 Men at Arms were drafted to service. Each company was made up of the three knights, 24 men at arms.

In September the garrison was again built on with the arrival of a contingent of Irish forces made up of 15 Hobelars and 40 Infantry along with these are two Troops of English Infantry; the first one of 160 arriving on 20 September. The other company of 20 arrived four days later.

It is important to note that some that a small unit may have left Carlisle in november, this unit was made up of 2 Knights and 21 men at arms. With one of the knights returning. In addition to the build up.

With the ongoing issues of raids and sabotage ment that Carlisle would be provided with two more knights, three men-at-arms and a total of 115 Archers. The garrison at the end of 1314 the forces in and around Carlisle; nine knights, 87 men-at-arms, 45 Hobelars and 395 foot soldiers.

Separate to the improvement of the garrison was the growing issue, that would be rock of the whole European. Due in large part to a very wet summer. The food crop rotted in the fields as none of the crop was brought in. This would eventually cause huge famine across Europe as there was also very limited crop seed.

Chapter 9 1315.

Much of what we know of the siege comes from the Lancoast Chronicle, which is a long lasting document that was written between 1201 to 1346. And covers the Wars of Scottish Independence.

Robert the Bruce had brought an army to take both the city of carlisle, Roberts army had always used speed and surprise to take castles but with Andrew and the gassion were waiting and watchful. The only experience that the Scottish army had was the siege of Stirling castle Which meant that Robert had no choice but to utilize conventional methods of siege warfare.

Siege warfare is a form of warfare that seeks to force a "stronghold" to capitulate by any means required. In the modern age this is most often by Storm (such as in the Iran Embassy), or by negation. Conventional siege of the medieval was a slow affair.

On Robert's side; he had an army that some have estimated of being around 8,000, the army had constructed classical equipment for this type of siege.

The Scottish army brought with them the equipment for the siege, which included ladders, equipment of mining, portable bridges, and stone throning siege engine (thought to be a trebuchet) and a Berefrai or more commonly known as a siege tower.

On the English side, was the army of Carlisle Andrew Harclay commanding, to support the defense the English had stopped up the gates. And had built a small number of springald, Between seven and eight stone throwing engines.

The castle and the city had been prepared by stopping up or filling in some of the city gates' houses and by pulling down the building just outside the city walls to make it more.

According to the Lancoast Chronicle the siege itself starts on the 22nd July 1315, the army of scotland first tried to use the strategy of guile and speed that had worked in the past.

The first set of attacks were centered around the gatehouses, but these seem to be unsuccessful. On the 30 or 31st of July the Huge General attack tested most of the defenses around Carlisle. The hardest fighting was at the southernmost gate (also known as the Botchergate) the Black Douglas (Sir James Douglas) with a small unit of elite fighters. Made it over the walls but while met with some success was met by defenders and were driven back.

The Siege was not broken by any counter attack, but by the whispers that ran wild, when an army was cold, wet, bored, hungry and disaffected. The rumor was that there was a huge army led by the English king (Edward II).

Maybe Robert believed there was an army, maybe not. But nevertheless Robert marched his army away. We now know there was no army coming to Carlisle to break the siege.

With the end of the siege comes an end to the threat of invasions while there are raids into England. The Scots don't attack Carlisle for some time. The victory was seen as a massive success by the establishment.

Andrew was rewarded with power, land and fame, Andrew from a moderately privileged had broken the glass ceiling in becoming a member of the elite.

While this was going on in the background the huge failure of the Harvests.

The Aftermath

After the siege had taken its toll and the issues, are the detailed reconstruction efforts, paired with the needs of manpower, supplies and money.

However, the formal state of war would continue between the crowns of England and Scotland. There was a need for military activity though military patrols. Andrew would be captured the following year in the first part 1316 and kept prisoner by the scots.

The scots ransomed Andrew back to the english, at the price of 2000 Marks, the Meteoric rise of sir Andrew along with success had brought him political opponents at the royal court, i suspect that these are supporters of the lords that were supplanted to provide andrew with his rewards and lands.

This having been said, even King Edward II supported the efforts to arrange the knights' freedom. But the political moths had eaten away at the fabric of Andrew's reputation. Andrew would seem to lose his position as sheriff and would not return to the role until 1319.

While Andrew was away, great energy had been put into providing for the defense and supply of Carlisle, though imports from Ireland built up both a supply of food and drink. The Central government of the royal court supported the supply and equipment of troops. But there seems to have been a dislike for maintaining defense infrastructure in the north of england.

Andrew would serve with distinction at the battle boroughbridge; this was due to the attempted insurrection of Thomas of Lancaster. This was over the lack of focus (of the king's attention), on the ongoing war with scotland.

After attempting to create a rebellion which had little to no support, in March of 1322 he and his army were fleeing north. With the king in hot pursuit. Edward sent a message to Andrew (who was still sheriff of westmorland) in order to call all forces of westmorland and march south.

While resting the army at Ripion, Yorkshire (yes the one the TV show[2]), receives a message that Thomas of Lancaster, and his army were close by and attempt to cross the bridge at Boroughbridge the following day.

Seizing the initiative, Andrew captures the bridge and on the 16th of March 1322, sights the enemy. Andrew's army numbered around four thousand men. Thomas of Lancaster only had around 700 Knights and Men-at-arms.

Andrew set his army the Northern side on the bridge, with a small unit sent to defend ford close by. The army utilized the Schiltron formation, to defend the north side of the bridge.

The Oppantenting army, split into two units the first was led by Hereford and Roger de Clifford, and a second one commanded by Thomas of Lancaster. Thomas' opening move was to send his first company across the bridge to push Andrew Back, but it didn't work. In this advance Hereford is killed and Robert de clifford is seriously injured, thus the attack fails.

Thomas then leads his forces across the bridge but then sends his Heavy Cavalry to the ford mentioned earlier. However, Andrew's troops stationed at the crossing managed to restrain the Caverly.

All three attacks having failed, Thomas retires from the field under truce to a local town, that night there is a mass desertion. The next day the

---

[2] The Town in Rippin was Mentioned in the TV show Downton Abbey.

banners of the sheriff of york are seen and the heavily outnumbered Thomas of Lancaster Surrenders to Andrew.

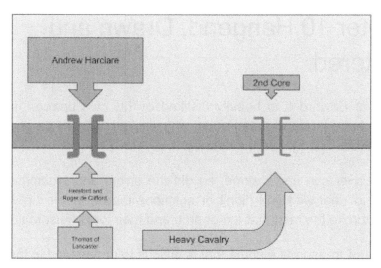

A Hugely Simplified map of the Battle

Thomas of Lancaster was taken to Pontefract Castle, where he was convicted in a single session (many sources claim that it was a show trial). Thomas was beheaded at the castle along with.

Andrew returns to Carlisle a hero, raised to the position of earl, the first earl of Carlisle. With this comes new investments of land which influence and power.

The total weight of feeling was starting to move against Edward II, it was not one thing, their general unfeeling for the affairs of state, this also paired with an inability to perform on the battlefield and in the field of war.

This built to a critical mass where many Magnates and lords, came to the relation that the king could not be trusted with the crown, which would lead to Edward II deposed in mid to late January 1327. We will the single thing that drove Andrew To commit the most heinous crime of the time, Treasion.

Chapter 10 Hangend, Drawn and Quartered.

To say that Edward II is heavily disliked by his own barrons, and while there is a huge amount written about why disliked. But any personal failing in the methods used to run the country.

Just as a river can carve stone, so did the errors and problems that the king had to deal with and didn't or solutions that he came up with didnt work, this broke the trust that a monarch and their lords must maintain.

The crime of treason is a crime that is difficult to understand in the modern age as Treason while still existing as law, but has not been used since 1945 (the case of William Brooke Joyce). At the time of writing only a member of the Privy Council and accuse any person of Treason in the UK.

The legal definition that was current in the early 1300s, had many nuanced parts, The part that is important is the concept of petty Treason.

Petty Treason for the sake of this document is any act that moves or seems to move against the declared wishes of the crown. Taking in the conditions as explained in Chapter one. We can see why this very hard and fast definition is required.

Because the context is so important to Andrew's Treason it important to provide a list of the most important points;

- The failure of crops on both sides of the border weakens the ability of both sides to continue active Warfare.

- While Carlisle was getting food from Ireland, it is clear from the context that food shipments were open to attack.
- The faith and trust in the crown had been damaged and one rebellion had happened already, with no reason to expect that was the end, opening the possibility of fighting a war on two fronts.

It was in this context that Andrew reached out in secret to begin negotiations with Robert the Bruce. Even in modern times the idea of diplomatic backchannels are well utilized.

The straw that broke the horse's back came on 14 October 1322 Robert the Bruce routed an English army at the Battle of Old Byland. So complete was the routing that the Commander (John of Britianainy, the earl of Richmand) was captured.

The king was 15 miles away (four hours march approximately), when the Earl of Richmand was defeated. In response Edward flew to York abandoning both land and the great seal of England (the seal is what charters, laws and other documents the Authority of the crown.), Andrew himself was on the march, coming to support the crown. But he could not make it in time.

Because of this Andrew is suspected of then entering into direct negotiations with Scotland, both coming to equitable agreement and sealing the treaty in January of 1323. The treaty agreed the following;

- Scotland to be an independent country.
- Robert was to pay 40,000 marks.
- Edward would have the right to choose the wife of the person who was Robert's successor.

There is a theory that this was an opening for Andrew to defect to the forces of Robert the Bruce, but I feel this is unlikely given that Andrew had spent almost his entire professional career fighting the scots. I personally think that Andrew was trying to depressurize his situation with Scotland and prepare for a number of conflicts in England.

It is wholly unlikely that Andrew expected to receive clemency for his actions, but when Edward II finds out about the peace treaty, he immediately calls for Andrew to be arrested and tried.

Edward Sends north Lord Anthony de Lucy the High Sheriff of Cumberland, who on or around the 25th of February 1323 arrests Andrew at Carlisle Castle. And was held on till been seen by a royal justice on the 1st March.

Andrew was brought into court wareing his robes of state, and was not granted a fair hearing, Andrew had the spurs hewn (cut) from him, and his sword broken by striking him around the head. And then he is stripped of his royal vestments.

The court proclaims Andrew to be no knight but a Knave (a person not worthy of trust.) he then sentenced to a gruesome death at the hands of royal executioners, the method was the same fate of William Walce.

Hanged. Drawn and Quartered was the worst way to die of its day, you are not just killed you are destroyed both body and soul. One is taken to the scaffold, and hung until one is half dead (past resistance).

The executioners then take them down, and place them onto a table or bench; this is where he was Emasculated, then Disembowelled, beheaded, and finally Quartered.

In the case of Andrew his head was taken to the lap of the king In Knaresborough, and then was taken London, the Quarters were "displayed" in Carlisle, Newcastle, Bristol and Dover.

While many people will respond to facing their own death in a variety of ways, in this Andrew Proved his own nobility. To a crowd he did not plead for mercy, he didn't ask for deliverance, nor did he ask for forgiveness. He simply said that he had acted in the interest of protecting his own people.

Five years later Isabel Andrew's sister who had been a ward of the king, petitioned the king to have the parts of Andrew returned to Isabel and Andrew be permitted a christian burial.

While it seems that Andrew is vindicated by history is that Edward signs a 13 year peace settlement with robert the bruce just three months after Andrew execution. With this brings to a close the Life of the knight, the Soldier and statesman Andrew Harcla. Which also poses one final question: where is this man buried.

In the work of Conelius Nicholson, there is an account of works being conducted on the church at Kirkby Stephen, where they find an unmarked grave in a filled archway. This theory concludes that this is the final resting place.

Andrew was a soldier, a knight and a statesman, who is partly forgotten in history, but even in my own small way to write about a man who fought with bravery and conviction. But also carried for the people he is interested with there welfare.

Works Cited

"Andrew Harclay, 1st Earl of Carlisle." *Wikipedia*,

   https://en.wikipedia.org/wiki/Andrew_Harclay,_1st_Earl_of_Carlisle.

   Accessed 8 September 2023.

"Battle of Bannockburn, 1314 AD ✕ First War of Scottish Independence

   (Part 5)." *YouTube*, 17 November 2019,

https://www.youtube.com/watch?v=TlcZWz0qykQ. Accessed 14

    September 2023.

Blackstone, William. "High treason in the United Kingdom." *Wikipedia*,

    https://en.wikipedia.org/wiki/High_treason_in_the_United_Kingdom.

    Accessed 10 September 2023.

"Blood of Bannockburn." *YouTube*, 16 May 2019,

    https://www.youtube.com/watch?v=YqqQq6L-JNc. Accessed 14

    September 2023.

Connolly, Matthew, and Isaac Taylor. "Isabel (Harcla) Vernon

    (abt.1261-aft.1329)." *WikiTree*,

    https://www.wikitree.com/wiki/Harcla-2. Accessed 14 September

    2023.

Cotterill, Simon, and Tom Hartley. "Hartley Castle." *Co-Curate*,

    https://co-curate.ncl.ac.uk/hartley-castle/. Accessed 14 September

    2023.

Douglas, William. "James Douglas, Lord of Douglas." *Wikipedia*,

    https://en.wikipedia.org/wiki/James_Douglas,_Lord_of_Douglas#Fi

    nal_campaign. Accessed 6 September 2023.

Editors, Charles River, et al. *Warfare in the Middle Ages: The History of Medieval Military and Siege Tactics*. CreateSpace Independent Publishing Platform, 2015.

Ferguson, Richard S. "Carlisle Castle." *Archaeology Data Service*, 1876, https://archaeologydataservice.ac.uk/library/browse/details.xhtml?recordId=3194120&recordType=Journal. Accessed 6 September 2023.

Gies, Joseph, and Frances Gies. *Life in a Medieval Castle*. HarperCollins, 2015.

"Hartley Castle." *Wikipedia*, https://en.wikipedia.org/wiki/Hartley_Castle. Accessed 14 September 2023.

Henninger, Mark G., and Raymond Edwards. "Henry of Harclay." *Wikipedia*, https://en.wikipedia.org/wiki/Henry_of_Harclay. Accessed 14 September 2023.

"Henry of Harclay (c. 1270–1317)." *Encyclopedia.com*, https://www.encyclopedia.com/humanities/encyclopedias-almanacs-transcripts-and-maps/henry-harclay-c-1270-1317. Accessed 14 September 2023.

Lancaster, Andrew. "Sarah (Harcla) Leybourne (abt.1292-aft.1327)." *WikiTree*, 23 December 2022,

https://www.wikitree.com/wiki/Harcla-6. Accessed 14 September
2023.

McCarthy, M. R., et al. *Carlisle Castle: A Survey and Documentary History*.
Historic England, 2013.

Nicholson, Conelius. *Sir Andrew De Harcla, a personal episode in english
history*. J.W. Braithwaite, 1900s.

"Sarah de Harcla." *Wikidata*, 2 January 2023,
https://www.wikidata.org/wiki/Q76084220. Accessed 14 September
2023.

"Sir Robert Leybourne (1290–1327) • FamilySearch." *FamilySearch*,
https://ancestors.familysearch.org/en/LHJD-YFB/sir-robert-leybourn
e-1290-1327. Accessed 14 September 2023.

Sorkin, Arron, creator. *The West Wing*. 2003. Performance by Martin
Sheen, Warner Bros., 2003.

Traquair. *Freedom's Sword*. HarperCollins, 2000.

"Treason." *Wikipedia*, https://en.wikipedia.org/wiki/Treason. Accessed 10
September 2023.

"Treason Act 1842." *Treason Act 1842*,
https://www.legislation.gov.uk/ukpga/Vict/5-6/51/enacted?view=plai
n. Accessed 10 September 2023.

Printed in Great Britain
by Amazon

40833535R10030